What Can Rabbit Hear?

ring ring

Lucy Cousins

This is Rabbit.
He has big ears
so he can hear
well.

What cun Rabbit hear in the flowers?

buzz

buzz

What can Rabbit
hear in the sky?

What can Rabbit hear in the field?

baa baa

What cun Rabbit hear on the pond?

quack   quack

tweet
tweet

What can Rabbit hear in the tree?

What can Rabbit hear at bedtime?

quack quack

First published as *What Can Rabbit Hear?*
Republished as *What Can Pinky Hear?*
This edition published as *What Can Rabbit Hear?*
First published 1991 by Walker Books Ltd
87 Vauxhall Walk, London SE11 5HJ
This edition published 2005

2 4 6 8 10 9 7 5 3

Printed in China

British Library Cataloguing in Publication Data:
a catalogue record for this book is
available from the British Library

ISBN-13: 978-1-84428-662-1
ISBN-10: 1-84428-662-2

www.walkerbooks.co.uk